Not A.B

What Happens When We Die?

Carolyn Nystrom

ILLUSTRATED BY EIRA REEVES

ISBN: 0–8024–7855–7

Designed and created by
Three's Company, 5 Dryden Street,
London WC2E 9NW
Worldwide co-edition organized and
produced by Angus Hudson Ltd,
Concorde House, Grenville Place,
London NW7 3SA
fax +44 181 959 3678

Printed in Singapore

Moody Press, a ministry of the Moody
Bible Institute, is designed for
education, evangelization, and
edification. If we may assist you in
knowing more about Christ and the
Christian life, please write us without
obligation: Moody Press, c/o MLM,
Chicago, Illinois, 60610.

Do you ever think about dying? I do.
And my thoughts are quiet, sad, scary
thoughts.

Once when I was playing in our living room, a tiny brown bird flew straight at the window. It hit the glass with a thud and fell to the ground. For a few minutes it fluttered, then it lay still. I started to cry. I wanted the bird to get up and fly again. I waited, but it didn't move, so I ran outside and picked it up. I wanted to help it fly. But the bird lay still in my hand. I yelled for Mom.

4

Mom looked sad too. "The bird is dead," she said. "We have to bury it in the ground."

"No! No!" I yelled. "I want to keep it in my room. Maybe it will live again."

"That won't happen," Mom said quietly.

So Mom and I found a little box. We put soft cloths in the bottom. As I put the bird inside, a small feather clung to my finger. I put the feather in my pocket.

Then we dug a hole in our garden. We set the box in the hole and covered it with dirt. I found a pretty stone to mark the place.

5

Later, I sat holding the feather and thought long, long questions about death.

—**How long does being dead last?**

—*Does God want people to die?*

—*Will my mom still be my mom in heaven?*

—*Will I die some day?*

—*Does it hurt to die?*

—*WHERE IS HEAVEN?*

—*WHY DID I HAVE TO PUT THE BIRD IN THE GROUND?*

—**What will happen to it there?**

—*Will I see the bird in heaven?*

—*Why do birds and animals and people die?*

—*How could I go to heaven if my body is in the ground?*

They were hard, sad, scary questions. I cried a little for the bird that died. My mom sat beside me. She said, "It's all right to cry, Jenny." Then we talked about my questions.

Mom began by telling me again the story of God's making the world.

The world was beautiful then—perfect—with trees, flowers, animals, even little birds. Next, God made a man out of the soil of the ground. Then He made a woman out of a small bone from the man. He let the man and woman live in that beautiful place. During the day they took care of the plants and animals. In the evening God walked and talked with them. God said, "You may have everything here except one tree. If you eat fruit from that tree, you will die."

At first the man and woman wanted to obey God, but they became more and more curious about the special tree. The woman thought, *Perhaps God did not really mean what He said.* So one day she ate fruit from the tree. She gave some to her husband, and he ate too.

9

Romans 5:12–20; 8:18–23

The man and woman had disobeyed God; the world was no longer perfect. Ever since that time, every man, woman, plant, or animal that lives eventually dies.

Acts 2:22–24; 2 Corinthians 5:21

But God does not want His people to be dead forever. So He sent His Son, Jesus, to make up for the wrong that first man and woman had done. Jesus lived. But He was different from any other man who lived. Jesus never disobeyed God. Then Jesus died. But His death was different too. JESUS CAME BACK TO LIFE!

When an animal dies, its body stops moving. It can't see or hear or feel anything anymore. It can't breathe. Its heart doesn't beat. At first its body may look alive even though it is quite still. But in a few days it will begin to soften and smell bad. The body slowly turns back into soil. That is why we bury dead animals in the ground.

When a person dies, the same thing happens to his body. That's why we bury it in a cemetery.

We feel sad and sometimes we cry because we feel lonely without that person who died.

But a person is more than a body. Inside is the "really me," the part that thinks and feels and loves and makes me different from any other person in the world. That is called the soul.

As soon as one of God's people dies, just as quick as you can blink your eyes, that soul goes to heaven to be with Jesus. There he can think and feel and love, and play, and even work. And he is perfectly happy, because he is with Jesus. And Jesus has made his place in heaven just exactly what that person likes best.

15

Later, God will even make his body new and take it to heaven also. It will look a little like his old body that was buried in the ground, but the new body will be perfect—just like heaven. It will not be broken or hurt or sick or ugly.

Because Jesus came to earth and died and came back to life, we can live forever in heaven with Him. And forever doesn't ever end.

John 14:1–19

When Jesus was about to die, His friends felt sad. They knew they would be lonely after Jesus was gone. But Jesus said, "Don't be sad. I am going away to make heaven ready for you. But someday I'll come back and take you to heaven with Me."

We don't know exactly what heaven is like or even where it is. The Bible says that heaven is too wonderful for our minds to understand. But it is fun to imagine what Jesus might be preparing for us. Close your eyes and try.

20

Think of the most beautiful thing you have ever seen. Was it a mountain? A field full of wild flowers? A sunset? A basketful of baby puppies? Or something totally different—something no one but you would think is beautiful?

Now open your eyes. Heaven is even more beautiful than that.

Think again. When have you felt happiest in your whole life? On a trip to the zoo? On Christmas morning? Catching raindrops on your tongue? Or sitting quietly and holding your favorite pet?

You will be happier than that in heaven.

What do you like to do more than anything else? Play football? Ride a train? Swim? Bake cookies? Swing high on a tire swing? Lie on your back in tall grass and watch the clouds?

What would you choose to do if you were able to do anything you wanted? Would you pilot an airplane? Drive a fire truck? Take care of sick animals in a pet hospital? Maybe you would fly from here to Mars and build a city there.

In heaven you will do things even more wonderful—and you will enjoy them even more.

Think of your favorite person—someone you love more than anyone else. But do you sometimes get angry and want her to leave you alone? Or do you worry that she doesn't like you as much as you like her? Do you sometimes wish you could say what you really feel to that person—only the words don't come out right?

In heaven you can know that person perfectly. She will know you too. And you will love each other all the time.

In heaven you'll meet lots of other people too. You'll know and love God's people who lived a long time before you were born—like your great-great-great-grandmother and King David and the apostle Paul. And all of you will know Jesus.

Jesus will take care of you in heaven.

"But, Mom," I asked, "will the bird that died today be alive in heaven?"

"I don't know, Jenny." Mom was quiet for a moment. "But Jesus is making heaven perfect for you. If you still want that bird when you go to heaven, I'm sure the bird will be there."

Mom left then. I sat for a while looking at my feather, but my thoughts weren't so sad and scary anymore. I think I'll keep that feather on my dresser.